THAT'S WHY WE SING

RECLAIMING THE WONDER OF CONGREGATIONAL SINGING

Darryl Tippens

LEAFWOOD
PUBLISHERS

This booklet is an expansion of Chapter 12, "Singing: The Way to Heaven's Door," from *Pilgrim Heart: The Way of Jesus in Everyday Life* (Abilene, TX: Leafwood Publishers, 2006).

The author expresses his appreciation to several who read drafts of this essay and offered helpful suggestions, including Ken L. Adams, C. Leonard Allen, Everett Ferguson, Randy Gill, Kelly Neill, and Jack Reese.

That's Why We Sing
Reclaiming the Wonder of Congregational Singing

LEAFWOOD
PUBLISHERS

Copyright 2007 by Darryl Tippens

ISBN 978-0-89112-507-5

Printed in the United States of America

Cover design by Rick Gibson

For information contact:
Leafwood Publishers, Abilene, Texas
1-877-816-4455 toll free
www.leafwoodpublishers.com

07 08 09 10 11 12 / 7 6 5 4 3 2 1

O sing to the Lord a new song;
sing to the Lord, all the earth.
Sing to the Lord, bless his name;
tell of his salvation from day to day.

PSALM 96:1

THAT'S WHY WE SING

*Be filled with the spirit, as you sing psalms and hymns
and spiritual songs among yourselves,
singing and making melody in your hearts. . . .*
—Ephesians 5:18-19

Next to the Word of God, music deserves the highest praise.
—Martin Luther

When I think of my most memorable moments in church, the times I have felt closest to God, almost always they involve hymns. When I was a small boy, I recall my mother going forward to receive Christ in baptism, as we sang:

> Trust and obey,
> For there's no other way
> To be happy in Jesus
> But to trust and obey.

Whether it was through exuberant gospel songs in Sunday worship, devotional songs around a campfire, or Christmas carols sung heartily with family and friends—the joy of divine love and the wonder of forgiveness reached my head and my heart largely through music. The repertoire was large. There is a good distance between "Bringing in the Sheaves" and

"O Sacred Head Now Wounded," but all kinds of singing affected me deeply, permanently. I have come to see that I am not exceptional in this respect. In fact, the number of people who have been radically changed by sacred song is quite large.

In her highly original autobiography, *Traveling Mercies*, Anne Lamott tells the story of how she came to faith. In a period of despair, when she spent long, lonely days in a fog of alcohol, speed, and cocaine, spiraling towards destruction, something utterly unexpected occurred. During this dark time she visited a flea market in Marin City, California; and there she passed by a small, sad, ramshackle church building from which she heard the most remarkable music. She called it "glorious noise." At the time, Lamott was hostile to Christianity. She could not bear to hear a sermon, but the music drew her in, and she returned for more in the following weeks. The singing, she said,

> was furry and resonant, coming from everyone's very heart. There was no sense of performance or judgment, only that the music was breath and food. Something inside me that was stiff and rotting would feel soft and tender. Somehow the singing wore down all the boundaries and distinctions that kept me so isolated. Sitting there, standing with them to sing, sometimes so shaky and sick that I felt like I might tip over, I felt bigger than myself, like I was being taken care of, tricked into coming back to life.[1]

One Sunday in April, 1984, Lamott attended the church again. She stayed for the sermon that day, which she found unimpressive, but the music was mesmerizing:

> The last song was so deep and raw and pure that I could not escape. It was as if the people were singing in between the notes, weeping and joyful at the same time, and I felt like their voices or something was rocking me in its bosom, holding me like a scared kid, and I opened up to that feeling—and it washed over me.[2]

According to Lamott, "it was the music that pulled me in and split me wide open."[3] That day she decided she would become a Christian.

It would be hard to find a story that more vividly illustrates the power of music to enthrall and move a person to action. Through the centuries, music has been a primary means of conversion and spiritual formation, and it is happening today in a surprising way.[4] For most believers, music is not a frill or an ornament, not some illustration of a theological truth; much more, music is the good news in word and sound, the purest and most potent expression of God's presence and transcendence, and the best way to engage our hearts and imaginations, our bodies and souls.

Karl Barth, the great theologian, once wrote, "The Christian community sings. It is not a choral society. Its singing is not a concert. But from inner, material necessity it sings. Singing is the highest form of human expression....We can and must say quite confidently that *the community which does not sing is not the community*"[5] (my emphasis). We know in our hearts the truth of the theologian's insight—that Christians at worship must praise God with their lips in order to be the people of God. Full-voiced, vigorous congregational singing is central to the identity and mission of the church of Jesus Christ.

Yet something fundamental is happening to congregational singing in our day. It is at risk of dying out in some religious communions. The leaders of various churches which have long practiced congregational singing report that the practice is waning. Whole congregations are forgetting to sing; they are forgetting *how* to sing; and they are forgetting how to pass on a three-thousand-year-old legacy that reaches back to the practice of ancient Israel and the churches of the first century.

Vigorous, powerful singing can be preserved, but it will not happen primarily through argument. Rather, fervent *practice* will win the hearts of worshipers. One of the most passionate advocates of *a cappella* congregational singing is the distinguished Mennonite musicologist Mary Oyer. She says:

We have a wonderful heritage. I think we will keep it only if we sing. We have to sing much more. We have to practice by doing it. Sing more. Keep singing. Sing. Sing. Sing. Sing before church. Sing during church. Sing after church. Just do it.[6]

Mary Oyer understands that people's memories are short. If just one generation forgets how to sing, if just one generation misses the sheer joy of powerful congregational singing, preservation of the practice will be hard. If we lose vigorous, robust congregational hymn singing, we lose one of the church's greatest means of conversion, teaching, and spiritual formation.

If we are serious about preserving this venerable practice, we will learn why congregational singing is not merely a peculiar "identity marker" of our churches. Rather, we will understand it as an essential feature of a vibrant believing community. In the pages that follow, I wish to do two things: first, to recall some of the main reasons why singing is central in the life of the church; and, second, to offer some suggestions for its preservation and renewal.

SINGING CONNECTS US TO GOD.

People often change churches for surprising reasons. One reason is that church members are hungry for God. If they do not sense that God is present in worship, they become dissatisfied and look elsewhere. People want an *experience* of God, not just intellectual knowledge of him. This is not some postmodern aberration. It is the nearly universal cry of the human heart: "*O taste and see that the Lord is good!*" (Psalm 34:8); "*My soul longs, indeed it faints for the courts of the Lord; my heart and my flesh sing for joy to the living God*" (Psalm 84:2).

What do we have to offer these pilgrims in search of God? Hymn singing is an important part of the answer. Like the Psalms (which are, after all, hymn texts) our congregational hymns possess a unique capacity to address the human hunger for God. In mysterious ways sacred song connects the head and the heart, inspiring devotion, repentance, sorrow, joy, and reverence. Whether we sing "How Great Thou Art," "O Sacred

Head," or "I Come to the Garden Alone," the words and the music invite worshipers into the divine presence.

In the free church tradition, of which Churches of Christ are a part, a suspicion of sacrament and mystery is common. We have tended to emphasize *knowing* the right things (doctrine) and *doing* the right things (ethics and conduct). As one wit has put it, we're good at doing worship "from the neck up." Thinking, doctrine, and ethics are very important, of course; but we must admit the obvious: they alone are not sufficient to sustain our faith. One can know the right things, but falter. Our hearts cry out for more, a divine encounter. We want to enter Bethel (the house of God) and shout, "Surely, the Lord is in this place!" (Genesis 28:16). We don't just want *memories* of a God who once touched his creation; we want *communion* with him today.

If a sacrament is an earthly means to a divine encounter, then for many of us hymns have been our permissible sacrament. Hymns have provided a way to *feel* our faith and to express our heart's devotion to God. Though we may not use the word, the "sacrament" of song has long been our primary means of sacred contact. As we sing, we feel that God is present to us: "Yet thou art holy, enthroned on the praises of Israel," the Psalmist declares (22:3). We sense God's majesty, power, and splendor as we sing. Though this can also happen in prayer, Scripture reading, communion or a sermon, for many people it happens in music.

According to George Herbert, England's greatest devotional poet and an accomplished musician, church music is "the way to heaven's door."[7] Contemporary composers, worship leaders, and theologians make similar points. "Worship thrives on wonder," explains Matt Redman, who, with his wife Beth, authored the popular contemporary hymn "Blessed Be Your Name":

> We can admire, appreciate, and perhaps even adore someone
> without a sense of wonder. But we cannot worship without wonder.
> For worship to be worship, it must contain something of the other-
> ness of God.…[God] is altogether glorious—unequalled in splendor

and unrivalled in power. He is beyond the grasp of human reason—far above the reach of even the loftiest scientific mind. Inexhaustible, immeasurable and unfathomable—eternal, immortal and invisible.[8]

Christian hymns invite us to delight in God's presence, not merely think about him. Music awakens us to God's matchless power, beauty, and transcendence—his sheer otherness.

Without music we are left with talk. The trouble with talk is that it tends to position the speaker in a place of power. It puts one in charge, which can border on a dangerous conceit when it comes to reporting on the Almighty. A different, humbler posture of spirit emerges in worship and song. When we are singing, there is a sense that we are not in charge. The leading comes from the music—or it should. Anne Lamott's experience illustrates how we may submit to the power of the song (and therefore to the Spirit—the Reality—behind the music): "I felt like their voices or something was rocking me in its bosom, holding me like a scared kid, and I opened up to that feeling—and it washed over me." Music has this power to hold us, open us up, and bathe us. It happens *to* us. And when it is taken seriously—when it involves a whole-body immersion—it brings us to God.

SINGING CHANGES US.

Christianity is fundamentally about change, and singing changes us in extraordinary ways. How often have I entered the assembly distracted, out of sorts, or lonely; but in the singing, surrounded by a dozen voices, or a hundred, or a thousand, I have been mysteriously transformed. The power of congregational singing to move us has been eloquently described by a number of writers. In ancient times, Augustine of Hippo tells how singing played a major role in his decision to become a disciple. Addressing God in his *Confessions*, the great theologian writes:

How I wept during your hymns and songs! I was deeply moved by the music of the sweet chants of your Church. The sounds flowed into my ears and the truth was distilled into my heart. This caused the feelings of devotion to overflow. Tears ran, and it was good for me to have that experience.[9]

Singing doesn't just change us individually; it changes us collectively; indeed, it can change the world. Elie Wiesel, the Nobel laureate and survivor of the Holocaust, has written, "Through song…you climb to the highest palace. From that palace you can influence the universe and its prisons. Song is Jacob's ladder forgotten on earth by the angels. Sing and you shall defeat death; sing and you disarm the foe."[10]

SINGING INSPIRES FAITH.

When we believe, we sing. But often the action occurs in reverse order: First we sing, and then we believe. Belief doesn't just lead to song. Song leads to belief. How many millions of children first believed because they had been taught to sing, "Jesus loves me, this I know, / For the Bible tells me so"? In the simple act of singing, faith is silently, secretly born—or reborn.

Bill Henderson, novelist, publisher, and founder of Pushcart Press and the prominent Pushcart Prize, recounts a remarkable instance of the transforming power of hymns. One winter Sunday in 1990 Henderson found himself in his wife's church, where he had refused to attend. Though he had given up on Christianity, he decided to go to church with his wife that Sunday because a record blizzard had made the roads too treacherous for his wife and daughter to travel alone. He writes:

> …I walked through the church door into a mostly empty room….Only a dozen people who lived nearby had turned out. The minister carried us in song. Simple, tentative voices muffled by the snow on the roof. Outside it was silent—not a car, not a crow. We could have been in the Roman catacombs at the very start of it all. No organ propelled us, no piano. We sang as best we could, missing words, mashing notes, but confessing everything to each other in our unadorned voices, as the snow swirled around us.

I don't remember what hymn it was, but suddenly I was gasping for breath, overwhelmed by recognition. In our singing was the love I sought, as we all did. I knew then it was all right for me to be in this little building. Because of that song, and because of my daughter, Holly, singing next to me in her innocence and simplicity, I was back in the church of my father and my mother.

Six months later I was a member of that church, and years later I was asked to be an elder and accepted—a cranky, suspicious-of-cheap-doctrine elder, amazed at my title.[11]

Kathleen Norris, author of *Dakota* and *The Cloister Walk,* describes a similar experience. While attending worship and listening to Scripture being chanted, Norris reports:

[T]ears welled up in me, unexpected and unwelcome. I remembered how completely I had loved God, and church, as a child, and how easily I had drifted away as a young adult. I realized suddenly that I'd been most fortunate in being given another chance to encounter worship, in middle age, in a context that restored to me the true religion of my childhood, which was song.

Norris adds that she discovered that true religion "consists not so much of ideas and doctrines but of song and breath."[12] She remembers that when she was a child, she thought "singing was the purpose of religion."[13] If singing is not the sole purpose of religion, it is certainly one of its principal supports. Anyone serious about spiritual formation will give considerable attention to sacred music—the music of congregational worship, the music of youth groups and youth gatherings, the music that fills our homes and automobiles, the music that fills our lives.

Singing Connects Head and Heart, Body and Soul.

For those suspicious of emotion, music's power to take us where the intellect cannot go is alarming, but scriptural example should allay our fears. The fact that the Bible contains *hundreds* of song texts, many highly emotional in nature, tells us something important. Consider Mary's song of praise (Luke 1:46-55). It expresses more than doctrinal truths (though it does that). Song overflows in ecstasy as the virgin realizes she is to bear the Christ child. If we do not *feel* Mary's transport, if we do not sense the sheer surprise and wonder pulsating in her words of praise, then we are deaf to the glorious music in the text.

In similar fashion the great songs of the Old Testament (especially the Psalms) express strong emotion—exultant joy like Mary's, but also deep sorrow, brittle anxiety, raw fear, and luminous hope. The whole range of human emotion is captured in the Psalms, and this is precisely why we need them in our communal and private worship. The Psalms permit us, indeed *require* us, to be fully human before our fellow worshipers and before God. They dissolve our pretensions to having it "all together." They expose our "niceness" as the sham that it is. They demand truth from us—not just pious thoughts in our heads, but the full conviction and the passion of our hearts. Surely, if all the Psalms (not just a few favorites) were restored to the worship of the church, we would be a more authentic and faithful community.[14] Singing succeeds because it requires the full involvement of the whole person. There is no other act of worship that is so encompassing, so visceral.

Singing Connects Us To One Another.

Singing is one of the church's primary means to inspire and build community. On the night he was betrayed, Jesus sang hymns with his followers (Matthew 26:30; Mark 14:26). The community that sings together comes together in a remarkable way, as Paul suggests in Philippians 2. Singing builds solidarity like nothing else, as Don Saliers points out:

> In our present North American cultural context, the singing
> assemblies in our churches…are among the very few remaining
> places where words and music actually form human beings into
> a communal identity….[W]hen people meet to worship, public
> singing still offers formation in a shared identity. This identity
> flows out of an ancient story that continues to take on new life, in
> words and tunes that speak today. It gives voice to individual people
> in praise, lament, and need, but it does not leave them isolated,
> surrounding them instead with a great choir.[15]

We have seen how Anne Lamott found consolation and community in the congregational singing. When the church in ancient Milan suffered persecution, Augustine reports that Ambrose's hymns provided encouragement and hope to the oppressed believers. The fact is that when a congregation sings "Be Still My Soul," "Listen to Our Hearts," or "When Peace Like a River," it is mysteriously consoled and nourished in the same way spirituals comforted oppressed African-Americans in the days of slavery. James Baldwin expresses the power of gospel music in an old-fashioned revival:

> As the singing filled the air the watching, listening faces underwent
> a change, the eyes focusing on something within; the music seemed
> to soothe a poison out of them; and time seemed nearly to fall away
> from the sullen, belligerent, battered faces, as though they were
> fleeing back to their first condition, while dreaming of their last.[16]

Sacred song tells our story and, somehow, makes it all right, as it binds us together in love with our brothers and sisters in hours of transcendent joy and deepest sorrow.

Singing Proclaims the Good News.

Hymns are extraordinary because through their mysterious linking of body, emotion, and intellect, they plant the truths of the faith in our hearts, not just in our heads. Thus, hymns become remarkable tools of instruction. Doxologies, hymn fragments, and references to congregational singing run through Paul's letters.[17] The Apostle urges Christians to employ songs to teach, praise God, encourage one another, and express thanks: "Let the word of Christ dwell in you richly; teach and admonish one another in all wisdom; and with gratitude in your hearts sing psalms, hymns, and spiritual songs to God....[S]ing psalms and hymns and spiritual songs among yourselves, singing and making melody in your hearts...." (Colossians 3:16; Ephesians 5:19)

Hymns also rehearse the stories of Scripture. In word and melody we experience Gethsemane, the cross, and the resurrection. We remember our sinfulness, our need for redemption, our duty to our neighbor, and the promise of eternal life. In a time when people have a diminished capacity to absorb long sermons, hymns stand ready to offer important inspirational and didactic service to the church, as they have done for millennia.

Given the power of song to shape belief and move people to action, we should pay close attention to content. That which we sing, we tend to believe.[18] This can be a very good thing. In a theologically shallow environment, singing may redeem an otherwise impoverished service. As a youth I heard sermons that occasionally tended towards legalism or moralism, yet the service was full of songs like "Amazing Grace," "A Wonderful Savior," and "Love Lifted Me." The sermon may have been ensnared in law, but the music was rich in grace. In the same way, sometimes I heard sermons that warned against the dangers of excessive religious fervor, but then the congregation would stand and *fervently* sing:

When each can feel his brother's sigh,
And with him bear a part;

When sorrow flows from eye to eye,
And joy from heart to heart.

William Bradbury's stirring music and Joseph Swain's touching lyrics trumped the sermon of the day, for what we sing and feel in our hearts remains with us far longer than what we receive through passive listening. So it has always been, for hymns are "active theology."[19] According to Don Saliers, "the continuing worship of God in the assembly *is* a form of theology. In fact it is 'primary theology.'"[20] For this reason, we must pay close attention to the words in our songs, making sure that they are scripturally correct and theologically sound.

Paul understood the capacity of hymns to impart core spiritual truths. When he wished to encourage Christians to live sacrificial lives, he didn't limit his discourse to reasoned argument. Instead, he appealed to people's memory of worship, citing a familiar hymn, the great "Carmen Christi" or Song of Christ (Philippians 2:5-11). On other occasions the great missionary-evangelist quoted poetry or hymns to illustrate his message and move his readers or listeners to act (Ephesians 5:14; 1 Timothy 3:16; Acts 17:28).

Music is vital to faith because it is a primary aid to spiritual memory. Hearing a song from our childhood can instantly catapult us to a precise location and moment—when we were singing in church, on a mission trip, on a retreat, or in the school choir. The power of music to remind us of God's faithfulness is all to the good because spirituality presupposes, indeed demands, vivid recollection. Through music we remember.

Singing does many more things for us that cannot be discussed at length here. One of the virtues of singing is its simplicity and univer-sality. Kelly Neill, classical singer and vocal music professor, observes: "We can all sing without professional training. We don't have to bring an instrument, [for] the instrument is within us." He adds: "I love the linking of the words with the music and the slower speed of the words when sung, and what that does to our spirits and minds. I love the fact that everyone has a unique voice....The blending of all our individual gifts is a beautiful picture of the body of Christ."[21] Singing soothes troubled hearts and prepares us for heaven, where there will be lots of singing. According to Kathleen Norris, Revelation reminds us that "only the good remains, at the end….We will sing a new song. Singing and praise will be all that remains. As a poet, that's a vision, and a promise, I can live with."[22] A fair question might be: Until we assemble in that vast heavenly throng, how can we tune our lips and our hearts in the meantime? In remaining pages, I offer a few suggestions.

Preserving and Enhancing A Cappella Singing

Precisely because music is so important, we should not be surprised that anxiety is often aroused when a congregation contemplates changes in its worship. As we sort through the changes, everyone concerned needs an extra measure of patience and humility. The array of styles of church music is vast, yet most of us have been exposed to only a very limited spectrum. Thousands of hymns have been written over the last two thousand years, and only a few of these are known to us. If we turn to the Bible for guidance, we find that it never prescribes particular musical styles. Styles change, and no single era has an exclusive claim on musical excellence. Every age has its forgettable tunes and inadequate lyrics as well as its masterpieces, but even the mediocre ones may be vehicles of faith for some.

It is worth remembering that "[t]he meaning of music resides in people, not in sounds."[23] So, one's personal judgment of a song's worth may be quite off the mark. I recall traveling for a week through Israel, hearing Middle Eastern music emanating from automobiles, restaurants, and homes as we drove through Arabic, Jewish, and Druze neighborhoods. Was the music good or bad? I simply had no context to judge. Given everyone's limited experience of music, and given the extraordinary breadth of music available today—classical and contemporary, local and international, European and Eastern, Catholic and Protestant, mainstream and charismatic renewal—being slow to judge an unfamiliar or unappealing musical form is the charitable way.

We face a serious cultural challenge today. Never in history have humans had so much exposure to professionally produced music (virtually all of it instrumental). In earlier times, one could go a lifetime and not hear highly polished professional musicians. In rural America, music was largely produced by ordinary (amateur) members of the family, church, and school. Nearly everyone sang or played an instrument. One need not sing well, but everyone was invited to participate. Musical performance was not the special domain of the professional; rather, it was the routine practice of ordinary people.

Times have changed. We are less and less a *singing* culture, more and more a *listening* culture. We are surrounded, day and night, by professionally produced music. As we move from active participation to passive listening, an even more ominous consequence emerges. In a world of "American Idol," we become entitled judges of everyone's performance. In other words, we move from being singers to being listeners, then, finally, to being consumers and self-appointed critics. In such a consumerist world, congregational singing suffers. Instead of praise being understood as a sacrificial gift to God; it becomes a human performance subject to critical analysis. (What did you think of the singing this morning?) This may explain why some sit through the service, lips sealed. They do not feel qualified. They do not understand that through silence they are withholding a gift rightfully due their Maker and Lord. What can be done?

The fact is, we have some choices. We can recognize the historical and theological basis of *a cappella* singing. Church historians generally agree that early Christian worship was *a cappella*. James McKinnon's *Music in Early Christian Literature* and Everett Ferguson's *A Cappella Music in the Public Worship of the Church* attest to this fact.[24] *A cappella* singing remained common, even normative, in many churches through the eighteenth century, just as it continues to be normative for millions of Eastern

Orthodox believers, many Anabaptists (the Mennonites and the Amish), and Reformed Presbyterians.

Singing and Humility

Many of us reared in Churches of Christ have heard a number of arguments for *a cappella* singing that seem to carry far less weight than they once did. It is perhaps time to consider other ways of approaching the subject. Many of the old arguments were negative in nature—why instrumental accompaniment is wrong. I suggest that we would receive a better reception if we offered positive arguments for unaccompanied singing. One brilliant Christian from the ancient world—perhaps the greatest mind of the ancient church—was Augustine of Hippo. His understanding of *a cappella* singing could be helpful in our time.

Singing is vital because it is the means to expressing the otherwise inexpressible, Augustine maintains. Whether we feel ineffable joy or sorrow, songs are the heart's response to divine grace. Augustine said it like this: "Think of people singing as they go about some hot and exhausting job at harvest-time, say, or in a vineyard. They start celebrating in their happiness with the words of familiar songs. But they end up turning away from words and syllables, as if they were filled with so much happiness that they couldn't put it into words.…off they go into the noise of 'jubilation.' This kind of singing is a sound which means that the heart is giving birth to something it cannot speak of."[25]

In Augustine's words we find a clue to the early Christians' devotion to singing. They believed that sacred music should be a direct expression of the human heart. But can't a musical instrument do this just as well? Many would say so; but Augustine seems to argue otherwise. Commenting on one of the Psalms about instrumental music (Psalm 149:3—"Let them praise his name with dancing, making melody to him with tambourine and lyre"), Augustine draws a parallel—and a distinction—between making music with an instrument and making music with the human voice.

Many have often wondered: Since the early church made extensive use of the Psalms in worship, yet these same texts frequently mention instruments of music, why did the early church not follow the Old Testament example in using them? Augustine's commentary indirectly answers this question: Old Testament instruments stood as earthly symbols of something spiritual in Christian worship. In Augustine's terms, there is a "mysterious [i.e., spiritual or allegorical] meaning" to such passages. While moderns may not readily understand this "spiritual reading" of the Old Testament, it was a normative way early Christians read the Bible (as seen in Paul's letters and the Book of Hebrews, most notably). The church's "spiritual understanding" of Old Testament musical references lasted for centuries.[26]

Concerning Psalm 149:3 Augustine writes:

> We should not pass over the mysterious meaning of "tambourine and lyre" in silence. On a tambourine you have a skin stretched out, and in a stringed instrument you have catgut stretched out. So in both instruments ordinary flesh is "crucified." The man who said, "The world is crucified to me and I to the world" [Gal. 6:14] must have sung praises really well on this "tambourine and lyre"! *And he who loves a 'new song' wants to take you to be that lyre, that tambourine.* He gives you his instructions when he says, "Whoever wants to be my disciple, let him deny himself and take up his cross and follow me." (my emphasis)

Augustine is developing a moving and, as we shall see, a spiritually challenging analogy. According to Augustine and the early church, in the age of the New Covenant human beings are the instruments through which God makes his amazing music. The people of God no longer *play* tambourines or lyres; rather, they themselves *become* God's musical instruments. A striking thought. In Augustine's thinking, God is the musician and the people are his instruments. No tambourine or lyre ever plays itself. It is an empty, lifeless thing until the musician takes it up. We too are empty, lifeless instruments until God breathes his Spirit into us and gives us song (Ephesians 5:18-19; Colossians 3:16).

Augustine continues this line of thinking:

> Let them [the followers of Christ] be stretched out on the wood [of the cross], and all fleshly desire dried out of them. Strings or sinews sound more sharply the more they are stretched out. And what does Paul the apostle say about making his harp sound more sharp and clear? "Forgetting what lies behind and straining forward to what lies ahead, I press on toward the goal for the prize of the upward call" [Phil. 3:13-14]. So he [Paul] stretched himself out; Christ touched him, and the sweetness of truth gave tongue.[27]

Augustine is expressing an arresting thought: Christ, the master musician, "plays" the suffering follower of Jesus. Our sufferings are evidenced in the way he stretches us. Paul is his primary example. God touches the human lyre (the apostle) and sacred music emanates from him ("Christ touched him, and the sweetness of truth gave tongue.") God, the Great Musician, does the same to all who submit to him. God wants a "new song," and that new song is played upon and through the human heart and body. We become the stretched skins (like those Old Testament tambourines and lyres) that reverberate with the praises of God.

Such an analogy is challenging, for it implies that the music God wants is costly. Like other spiritual disciplines, making melody in our hearts involves self-renunciation and suffering. It is a sacrifice, which is, by definition, demanding. If we will submit to his painful stretching, God will produce an exquisitely sweet melody through us—but at some cost. This is the sacred song that fills the spheres: "Sing *from the heart* in gratitude to God" (Colossians 3:16). "Sing and make music *from your heart* to the Lord" (Ephesians 5:19, Revised English Bible, my emphasis).

This view of singing is humbling. We are not in charge; God is. The great music is not our achievement, but God's. (It flows from his indwelling Spirit.) Instruments do not play themselves; they are played by the musician. If we—the instruments—are out of tune, broken, or resistant, the music will not come forth easily.[28] Rather than judging how others sound, our primary focus should be on preparing our own instrument—our own hearts—for God's glorious music. How often have we expressed this very truth when we sang "Lord, We Come Before Thee Now," asking God to tune us:

> Lord, on Thee our souls depend:
> In compassion now descend;
> Fill our hearts with Thy rich grace,
> Tune our lips to sing Thy praise.

Short of radical submission to the will of God, there is no assurance that we will be God's instruments, that we will "make music" to his glory. In any discussion of church music, our own failure to be fitting instruments of God should be ever before our eyes. We should humbly sing, "*Lord, make us instruments of your peace....*"

"KEEP SINGING. SING. SING. SING."

Beyond argument, we should redouble our efforts to strengthen the practice of *a cappella* singing. Congregations that are truly committed to congregational singing will make singing a much more vibrant part of their church life. Lively, joyous practice will serve the goal better than polemical argument. Mary Oyer is right: "We have to sing much more. We have to practice by doing it. Sing more. Keep singing. Sing. Sing. Sing. Sing before church. Sing during church. Sing after church. Just do it."

A congregation that is not enthusiastic in its corporate praises of God is at risk of forfeiting the tradition. Sacred song flows naturally from souls on fire. When there's no fire, people look for some way to make up for the lack. Karl Barth observes that when a church "does not really sing but sighs and mumbles spasmodically, shamefacedly and with an ill grace, it can be at best only a troubled community which is not sure of its course, and of whose ministry and witness there can be no great expectation."[29] Consider a very different encounter with worship. A visitor described what it was like to hear a congregation sing psalms in Strasbourg in the 1540s:

> [F]or five or six days at the beginning, when I looked on this little company of exiles from all countries, I wept, not for sadness, but for joy to hear them all singing so heartily and as they sang giving thanks to God that He had led them to a place where His name is glorified. No one could believe what joy there is in singing the praises and wonders of the Lord in the mother tongue as they are sung here.[30]

The *a cappella* singing described here matches the kind of outpouring that Paul describes in the New Testament—joyous thanksgiving animated by the Spirit. If *a cappella* music falls on hard times in our day, it may not be because the form has fallen out of favor or because our arguments fail to convince, but because we are no longer singing in the Spirit, with gratitude at the wonders of the Lord (1 Corinthians 14:15).

Early Christian writers noted the extraordinary shaping force of singing on the worshiper. When the congregation praised God, they noted that the whole church was transformed. The singing provoked an amazing bounty of love and unity among the flock. Basil the Great says it like this:

> [Singing the psalms] settles one's tumultuous and seething thoughts....A psalm creates friendships, unites the separated and reconciles those at enmity. Who can still consider one to be a foe with whom one utters the same prayer to God! Thus psalmody provides the greatest of all goods, charity, by devising in its common song a certain bond of unity, and by joining together people into the concord of a single chorus.[31]

If our singing is authentic, it will inspire a spirit of love, kindness, and unity, Basil claims. A singing church inspires peace and compassion, not rancor or bitterness.

Churches deeply committed to *a cappella* music will give special attention to teaching their members—especially their young—to sing, to sing often, to sing well, and to do it in a way that is truly enjoyable. "Are any cheerful? They should sing songs of praise" (James 5:13). Many churches used to do this well, but have ceased to do so. While congregations commonly give attention to preaching, teaching, and youth ministry, they often fail to think creatively and imaginatively about how they can inspire their members to sing often, well, and vigorously.

It is not only the young who need to learn the songs; so do older members. Unfortunately, some song leaders alienate segments of the congregation because they fail to consider that many do not know the new songs. Many older members appreciate the new hymns, but they sometimes feel left out since no one took time to *teach* the new songs before making them a part of the worship service. (Compounding the problem, often there is no musical notation to give struggling worshipers any help.) The resulting alienation is unnecessary. In singing there is an intimate intertwining of the minds, hearts, and spirits of the worshipers. Singing is not only for God, it is *for one another*; but when a segment of the worshipers cannot participate because of basic unfamiliarity, the possibility of joyous transcendence is blocked. Worship would greatly benefit from a simple commitment to introduce new songs as a part of the church's teaching program.

Elders, ministers, youth ministers have all sorts of meetings, conferences, and associations, yet today few churches invest in programs that really teach everyone to sing. Where are the regional and national meetings devoted to enhancing congregational singing? How many Bible lectureships give special attention to teaching new hymns? Where is the Christian university willing to establish a Center for *A Cappella* Worship? Where do worship leaders meet to share their knowledge of hymns, their methods for teaching new songs and old? Who is helping to revitalize the singing in old churches, small churches? It has been said, "The Christian church was born in song."[32] Perhaps the church in our day will be *reborn* through song as well.

What else can we do to practice, celebrate, and honor sacred song? We can raise the quality of the music in our churches. Excellence in music, as in all things, is a desirable goal. How much better would our worship be if we asked a few basic questions like these, as we select the music:

1. Are the people taught? (Are the music texts theologically true? Is the language comprehensible and meaningful?)

2. Are the people inspired? (Does the music engage the emotions?)

3. Do the people receive balance? (Is dignity balanced by exuberance? Is joy coupled with reverence?)

4. Are the people joined in a sense of community? (Does the music encourage participation by the full assembly?)

5. Is there a sense of awe? (Would a visitor exclaim, based upon the conduct of the service, "God is really among you"? 1 Corinthians 14:25)

We can do something else. We can develop worship leaders who know the international range of sacred music. The variety of excellent Christian hymns from around the world is nothing less than astonishing, yet most of these are quite unknown in our churches. I think of new hymns being composed by a Christian composer in St. Petersburg, Russia; Mennonite hymns, some old, some contemporary; Taizé hymns from France; and indigenous hymns from Asia and Africa. It's unfortunate that in our supposedly global age, so many song leaders are unaware of the rich possibilities of hymnody. Of course, someone has to have the time and energy to learn this music and to teach it to the church. If music is as remotely important in spiritual formation as I am claiming, then developing knowledgeable worship leaders makes sense. Perhaps the day is not far off when congregations will devote as much attention to worship music as they do to the preaching or youth programs. There is great talent

among us. Let us encourage the composition of new hymns by our musi-
cally and poetically talented members.

If we are serious about preserving congregational singing, then there
is something else we will do. We will pay close attention to the acoustics
of our worship facilities. Church architecture today is often designed to
amplify what is being spoken or sung at the front of the worship space.
Inattention to the acoustics necessary for congregational singing is unfortunate, if not disastrous. Ironically, some of the people most committed
to congregational singing in theory construct worship facilities that ruin
congregational singing. If we are wise, our worship facilities will support
our commitment to congregational singing.

So, we must teach our young to sing; we must sing often; we must
offer the church beautiful songs, old and new; we must learn a larger array
of hymns, borrowing from the vast worldwide body of Christian hymns.
We must lay aside our petty disputes over matters of preference (praise
songs versus classic hymns) and styles of leading (a solo song leader versus a
team of song leaders), and come together for the greater good of the fellow-
ship. We must create worship spaces that allow the human voice to soar.

We do not have to do all of this perfectly. Even if we do not achieve
all these goals, even if our services lack something (as they sometimes
will), transformational worship is possible if it is practiced with sincerity,
grounded in Scripture, and filled with the Spirit. Sophistication is not the
goal. Passionate engagement is.

"THE WILD, HEROIC RIDE TO HEAVEN"

It is possible that the quest for the ideal hymn perfectly sung could
obscure the goal of meeting God in worship. George Ives was a church
musician and the father of the great American composer Charles Ives. The
father taught his son to respect the power of vernacular music. Concerning a
stone-mason who sang irritatingly off key, the father instructed Charles:

> Watch him closely and reverently, look into his face and hear the
> music of the ages. Don't pay too much attention to the sounds—for

if you do, you may miss the music. You won't get a wild, heroic ride to heaven on pretty little sounds.[33]

George Ives's counsel is a fine commentary on Ephesians 5:19. The singing that pleases God is the melody in the heart, not the tune on one's lips.

In the so-called "worship wars" too many people, trapped in futile debates about the "pretty little sounds," have sadly missed "the wild, heroic ride to heaven." If we would be but more patient and flexible, recognizing that our singing is a gift to God (and therefore not primarily about our preferences), then it would matter less whether the song selection matches our personal taste. Christian music is a simultaneous offering of our voices to God, a receiving of God's word to us, and a statement of our faith proffered to the world.

If we must err in one direction, a missional attitude is prudent. Like Luther we should advocate music that wins the hearts of the young and the untaught. The great hymn writer Ambrose observed that children in his day took pleasure in church songs. They regarded singing as "a kind of play, productive of more learning than that which is dispensed with stern discipline."[34] In the spirit of Ambrose we should make sure that our youngest find particular joy in the singing, for a special reason: Robert Wuthnow has noted that when children are exposed to religious music, they are more likely to take religion and spirituality seriously when they become adults.[35] This being so, we should remember the youthful Augustines and the troubled Anne Lamotts lingering in our doorways, waiting to be touched by the good news of God through song.

Singing may well be the most overlooked of all the spiritual practices. As I reflect upon my own spiritual journey, I realize that music has been teacher, encourager, and friend. I vividly recall the day in high school when I decided that I wanted to attend a Christian college, a decision that forever changed the direction of my life. That same day a college choir was performing in a church not far from where I lived, and a group from my church attended the evening services and the concert that followed. As the choir strode solemnly into the assembly, singing a hauntingly beautiful hymn, my heart melted. The music "dissolve[d] me into ecstasies" and brought "all Heav'n before mine eyes," as John Milton expressed it.[36] Although I can't recall the specific hymns sung that evening, the *effect* of that music remains with me to this day. I am no great singer, but that doesn't matter. I knew that evening that I wanted to be in a place where such music is possible. Words of faith set to music convert us, encourage us, console us, sustain us, and take us to heaven's door. There would be little discipleship or spiritual formation without psalms, hymns, and spiritual songs.

Notes

1 Anne Lamott, *Traveling Mercies: Some Thoughts on Faith* (New York: Pantheon, 1999), 48.

2 Lamott 50.

3 Lamott 47.

4 Robert Wuthnow shows that the arts, music in particular, are at the center of a revival of American Christianity. See *All in Sync: How Music and Art Are Revitalizing American Religion* (Berkeley: University of California Press, 2003).

5 Karl Barth, *Church Dogmatics, Volume IV, Part 3, Second Half.* Eds. G W. Bromily and F. W. Torrance (Edinburgh: T & T Clark, 1962), 866-67.

6 *From Lift Every Voice & Sing* (video), quoted in Marlene Kropf and Kenneth Nafziger, *Singing: A Mennonite Voice* (Scottdale, PA: Herald Press, 2001), 161.

7 His poem "Church Music" contains these lines: "Sweetest of sweets, I thank you: when displeasure / Did through my body wound my mind, / You took me thence, and in your house of pleasure / A dainty lodging me assigned....But if I travel in your company, You know the way to heaven's door." Louis Martz, ed., *George Herbert and Henry Vaughan* (Oxford: Oxford University Press, 1986), 56-57.

8 Matt Redman, *Facedown* (Ventura, CA: Regal / Gospel Light, 2004), 23-24.

9 Augustine, *Confessions*, trans. Henry Chadwick (Oxford: Oxford University Press, 1992), 164 (IX.vi.14).

10 Elie Wiesel, quoted in Kropf and Nafziger 149.

11 Bill Henderson, *Simple Gifts: Great Hymns: One Man's Search for Grace* (New York: Free Press, 2006), 15.

12 Kathleen Norris, *The Cloiser Walk* (New York: Riverhead Books, 1997), 218.

13 Norris 90.

14 Dietrich Bonhoeffer once exposed the false piety of Christians who are uncomfortable with the passionate nature of the Psalter; "in so doing they want to be even more spiritual than God is...." *Life Together; Prayerbook of the Bible*, eds. Gerhard Müller and Albrecht Schönherr, trans. Daniel W. Bloesch and James H. Burtness (Minneapolis: Fortress, 1996), 168.

15 Don E. Saliers, "Singing Our Lives," in *Practicing Our Faith*, ed. Dorothy C. Bass (San Francisco: Jossey-Bass, 1997), 192.

16 James Baldwin, "Sonny's Blues," *Classics of Modern Fiction: Twelve Short Novels*, ed. Irving Howe, 4th ed. (San Diego: Harcourt Brace Jovanovich, 1986), 634.

17 Saliers 183.

18 "[P]erhaps our prayer (worship) determines our belief (theology) more than our belief (theology) determines our prayer (worship)." C. Randall Bradley, "Congregational Song as Shaper of Theology: A Contemporary Assessment" *Review and Expositor* 100 (Summer 2003), 357.

19 Bradley 357.

20 Don Saliers, *Worship as Theology: Foretaste of Glory Divine* (Nashville: Abingdon, 1994), 15.

[21] Kelly Neill, e-mail to the author, March 24, 2007.

[22] Norris, *Cloister Walk* 220.

[23] J. Nathan Corbitt, quoted in Bradley 365.

[24] James McKinnon, *Music in Early Christian Literature* (Cambridge: Cambridge University Press, 1987); Everett Ferguson, *A Cappella Music in the Public Worship of the Church*, 3rd ed. (Ft. Worth, TX: Star Bible Publications, 1999) ; see also Ferguson, *Early Christians Speak: Faith and Life in the First Three Centuries*, 3rd ed. (Abilene, TX: ACU Press, 1999), 152-57; and Ferguson, The *Church of Christ: A Biblical Ecclesiology for Today* (Grand Rapids: Eerdmans, 1996), 269-72.

[25] Augustine, quoted in Rowan Williams, *The Wound of Knowledge: Christian Spirituality from the New Testament to Saint John of the Cross*, rev. ed. (Cambridge, MA: Cowley, 1990), 98-99. In the quotation, I have substituted the words "tambourine" and "lyre" for the less familiar (or less precise) terms "tabret" and "harp."

[26] For an artistic expression of the heavenly superiority of *a cappella* music in the Italian High Renaissance, see Raphael's painting of "*The Ecstasy of St. Cecilia*" (c. 1514-16). Cecilia, the patron saint of music, gazes into the heavens as a choir of angels sing *a cappella*. At her feet a variety of musical instruments lie broken. The painting may be viewed at <http://www.answers.com/topic/the-ecstasy-of-st-cecilia>

[27] Augustine, quoted in Williams 99.

[28] Dr. Ken Adams, Professor of Music, Oklahoma Christian University, points out: "The instrument possesses only potentiality, which only a musician can realize. There are two requirements: (a) the instrument must be technically sound—no broken strings or cracked skin; (b) the musician must have the capability of awakening the instrument." In Dr. Adams's analogy, we see the need to tune ourselves for God's service (for his music-making); but we also see that God, being the accomplished Musician, can make beautiful music even on a broken, deficient instrument (a human being marred by sin). "The limitations of the instrument," Dr. Adams notes, "can be overcome [by a superior musician] (we've all experienced it), but it is not easy, and it won't happen automatically." Ken L. Adams, e-mail to the author, 21 March 2007. The metaphor of the disciple as God's instrument appears in various biblical passages: we are "earthen vessels" made for his use (2 Corinthians 4:7); his "workmanship" (artifacts, "poems") created for good works (Ephesians 2:10), etc.

[29] Barth 866-77.

[30] Quoted by Nicholas P. Wolterstorff in "Thinking about Church Music," in *Music in Christian Worship*, Charlotte Kroeker, ed. (Collegeville, MN: Liturgical Press 2005), 3.

[31] Basil the Great, *Homilia in psalmum* I, 2, quoted in James McKinnon, *Music in Early Christian Literature* (Cambridge: Cambridge University Press, 1987), 65-66.

[32] Ralph Martin, *Worship in the Early Church*, 1964: 39; quoted in McKinnon, 12.

[33] Jan Swafford, *Charles Ives: A Life in Music* (New York: W.W. Norton, 1996), 88.

[34] *Explanatio psalmi* I, 9; quoted in McKinnon 127.

[35] Wuthnow 70-71.

[36] Milton, "Il Penseroso," lines 163-166.

THAT'S WHY WE SING

is adapted from the acclaimed book *Pilgrim Heart*.

Read this fresh and richly practical guide to the Christian spiritual life.

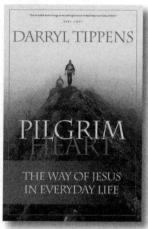